Mission, Risk & Suffering

Being lambs among wolves in a turbulent world

Matt Vaughan

First Edition 2015

Unless otherwise stated, Scriptural quotations in this publication are from the Holy Bible, Today's New International Version (TNIV)

Published by:
Kitab - Interserve Resources
5/6 Walker Avenue,
Wolverton Mill,
Milton Keynes
MK12 5TW
Email: sales@kitab.org.uk
www.kitab.org.uk

British Library Cataloguing in Publication Data
A catalogue record for this book is available from the British Library.

ISBN 978-0-9928610-2-5

Designed by Iain Gutteridge

Printed by Lavenham Press

This book is dedicated to my nephew Benjamin Hudson Vaughan
who was stillborn on March 28th 2012,
and who now rests in peace and safety with the Lord.

"Ye fearful saints, fresh courage take,
The clouds ye so much dread
Are big with mercy, and will break
In blessings on your head".

Light Shining Out Of Darkness, William Cowper, 1731–1800

Contents

Acknowledgement

I can vouch for the fact that Matt Vaughan tries to live out what he writes. He spots twin tendencies within western Christianity – a 'gospel of health and wealth' and a 'gospel of health and safety' – both issues reflecting our lack of a "theology of risk and suffering".

Hillsong Church, Sydney, is a remarkable church that, like many these days may identify with a "health and wealth" understanding of the Bible. However, this was tested recently when it held the funeral of Andrew Chan, an Indonesian whose family are members of the church. Chan was part of a drug smuggling ring "The Bali Nine" and was convicted, spending ten years on death-row, where he turned to Christ and became a pastor to others.

The church was praying for mercy for the convicted gang, reflecting the "risk-averse" mind-set of western Christians who have lost touch with the three Jewish teenagers in Babylon who said: '...but even if our God does not deliver us, we will not bow down' (Dan.3:16-18). When death by firing squad became a reality, it was the worst outcome for the church, but a release for the glory of God!

Why? – because eight of the Bali Nine turned to Christ, bringing gospel impact into the prison. Before the execution they refused to be blind-folded, choosing instead to hug one another, recite the Lord's Prayer and sing Matt Redman's song "10,000 Reasons".

Matt Redman called this 'the most profound act of worship ever' – as magazines carrying the story used the incident to promote Redman's next album.
(Source: Christian Today, Mark Woods, 08 May 2015)

It seems we do lack a "theology of risk and suffering" but this booklet is a valiant effort to help us put that right now.

Steve Bell
Series Editor

*'Jesus, all for Jesus,
All I am and have and ever hope to be.'*
- Robin Mark (1990 Word Music)

Author's Note

In 1838 a missionary named James Calvert was travelling to Fiji to plant a church among cannibals. When he arrived, the ship's captain begged him not to go, warning that he and his colleagues would be killed. Calvert replied: "We died before we came here" and got off the ship.

Today Christians in the western world are living at a time of unparalleled prosperity: high salaries, excellent healthcare, health and safety standards and levels of comfort unknown in the whole of history. We take for granted paid holidays, state-funded healthcare, pensions and social security; yet these seemingly mundane realities are actually incredible blessings which only a small percentage of the world's population will ever know.

Yet as we sit in comfort, we are surrounded by a world broken by injustice, war, and hunger, a world in which thousands die of preventable illnesses – a world of profound and deepening inequality.

God invites Christians to engage with him in this broken world; ignoring the invitation is not a valid option. It is in fact our command to: 'bring good news to the poor; to bind up the broken-hearted, to proclaim liberty to the captives'.[1] Yet doing this can be costly, time-consuming and even dangerous as it may lead to suffering.

James Calvert and his colleagues knew this when they got off the ship in Fiji. Their question is the question we face: *"Does the possibility of suffering prevent us from serving Jesus whole-heartedly?"*

> I work in a restricted Muslim country. When "home" to speak to supporting churches, I'm frequently asked: "Is it safe to work over there?"

The modern church in the western world is largely unequipped to cope with the problem of suffering. A primary cultural value is that difficulty is 'unnatural' while comfort, safety and the elimination of risk are prized as a 'right'; this has seeped into the church.

I work as a missionary in a restricted Muslim country and when I return "home" to speak to supporting churches, I am frequently asked: "*Is it safe to work over there?*" Before we even left for our placement overseas, a dear lady in a supporting church said: *"Don't be afraid. God may not protect all your possessions, but he always promises to protect your lives".* I was touched by her concern but I didn't have the heart to tell her that it's simply not true – in the Bible nor our personal experience.

---

1   *Isaiah 61:1*

Our own mission agency, Interserve, had just buried one missionary who died of a heart attack and two others who were killed in another country; two more would soon be murdered within the same year. I have heard others say things like: "God never gives us anything that we can't handle"; words which may not be a comfort to one lady we know whose husband was blown apart in front of her in a Taliban suicide attack on a church in Peshawar in September 2013. Too much of our understanding of 'discipleship' revolves around safety, well-being and *ourselves*.

For some western Christians, following Christ is as lukewarm and tedious as stale porridge; more of a lifestyle choice than a radical decision or than a commitment to the transformation of the world in Jesus' name. Which is more important: our own safety or the biblical injunction to be a witness for Christ throughout the world?

> Without a "theology of risk and suffering" we are incapable of responding well to the broken world which lies beyond our church doors.

We need a re-evaluation of the place of risk and suffering in Christian discipleship. The call is not to avoid risk, sitting in our cosy churches with the doors firmly shut against the prevailing storms of injustice and oppression that howl outside. It is a call to set aside our own well-being, as James Calvert did in 1830; and as so many unsung heroes of the Christian faith have done down the centuries. These stalwarts strode into the tempests of cruelty and inequality, while society insists we should 'play it safe', rather than hear Jesus' call to deny ourselves and take up our cross, and follow him.

Without a 'theology of risk and suffering' in Christian discipleship, we will be incapable of responding meaningfully to the broken world which lies beyond our church doors.

Please don't think that I'm trying to brow-beat western churches or to glorify suffering. We are not called to throw our lives away recklessly in the hope of being martyred. There is no difference between a so called, 'missionary' and any other line of work; we are all full-time Christian workers. Likewise, it's not necessarily better to work in a challenging urban setting than a proverbial 'leafy suburb'. What is crucial is that we are all called to follow Christ and to make him known.

The problem arises when we put our priorities before God's. If the possibility of suffering prevents you from following Jesus wholeheartedly, then it needs to be acknowledged. If this small book serves to jolt you (and me) into a richer and more abandoned form of discipleship, then it will have served its purpose.

Matt Vaughan
July 2015

ch **1**

Biblical Book-Ends

"I don't know if you've noticed it, but it's rummy how nothing in this world ever seems to be absolutely perfect".

The Inimitable Jeeves P. G. Wodehouse

© Wodehouse Estate, first published 1923 by Herbert Jenkins

The Bible "book-ends" human history between two focal points; these are the creation of the world in Genesis and the end of all things in the Revelation. We are living in the "middle times" between these points.

This means our lives are neither an endless stream of experience, as understood by some religious traditions; nor are we living in an ever-repeating cycle as understood by religious traditions such as Hinduism and Buddhism.

Our lives have a beginning and will have an end. At a point in history God created human beings and at another point in history the world and its inhabitants will come to an end. We are now living in between these two events. This changes everything and this is our starting point.

> The Bible book-ends history with two focal points – Creation and Revelation. We live in between these events, which changes everything!

In the Beginning

God didn't create an imperfect world. On the contrary: *"God saw all that he had made, and it was very good"*.[2]

This is a crucial starting point in coming to terms with risk and suffering. God didn't intend suffering to exist. His purpose was a world of perfection and peace; it was a love-gift from a loving God. Anything less than this would be inconsistent with the utterly loving character of God.

God never intended the world to include babies suffering and dying, nor terrorists who blow up buses; this is unthinkable and illogical. The Bible teaches that suffering came about due to our abuse of our God-given free will. As a result, the relationship between God, humankind and the earth was fundamentally fractured. The world in which we live is imperfect.

2   *Genesis 1: 31*

In the End

The Bible is equally clear about the end of the world. Nobody knows when this will happen – not even Jesus – but the Bible is clear that the end will come; and what an end it will be!

> *"And I heard a loud voice from the throne saying, 'Look! God's dwelling place is now among the people, and he will dwell with them. They will be his people, and God himself will be with them and be their God. He will wipe every tear from their eyes. There will be no more death or mourning or crying or pain, for the old order of things has passed away'"* [3]

This can transform our relationship to the world around us by helping us to hold more lightly onto that which is only temporary, knowing that no matter how dark human history and our own experience gets, 'perfection' awaits us. All the difficulties of the present pale into insignificance; as Paul writes: *"For our light and momentary troubles are achieving for us an eternal glory that far outweighs them all."* [4] So there will be a reunion of God, the redeemed of humankind and the earth. God will live among us and it will be blissful.

> **The profound message of the Revelation is that perfection awaits us if we will only hold on**

It's odd that so many writers analyse every minutiae of the book of Revelation – the meaning of the seven bowls; the identity of the Whore of Babylon; and what the Mark of the Beast might be. But the most profound message of the Revelation is this: perfection awaits us, if we will only hold on. The world began in perfection and it will end in perfection.

Here in the Middle Times

So here we are today, caught in the middle between these two bookends of time. We were created to express God's perfection and – one day – that perfection will be restored, but meanwhile we are in-between the two points in a world characterised by risk and suffering. It's an imperfect world of pain, violence, cancer, corruption, famine and suicide bombings. Notice the alternating evils – the natural order and human nature run amok as a result of the Fall.

The gospel is the good news that God has intervened in human history in-between the bookends of time. He did this in the person of Jesus Christ whose birth, death and resurrection started a revolutionary process of restoration of everything. The disruption caused by the Fall began a reversal in the great redemptive offering of Jesus on the cross. The rift between God, humankind

---

3   *Revelation 21: 3-4*
4   *2 Corinthians 4:17*

and the earth was restored; a fact reflected physically by the tearing in two of the dividing curtain of the Jewish temple in Jerusalem, signifying the renewing of fellowship with the creator.

The healing process is not yet complete. The complete transformation of the world order will be when we reach the final bookend. During these 'middle times' Jesus described the good news going global: *"And this gospel of the kingdom will be proclaimed throughout the whole world as a testimony to all nations, and then the end will come"*.[5]

We can expect nothing less than suffering and triumph during these middle times where we remain imperfect creatures, prone to temptation and sin. Meanwhile a battle rages on around us and within us. The tension is between our human nature and our divine calling – which will win? The Apostle John says: *"We know that we are from God, and the whole world lies in the power of the evil one"*.[6]

Because of Jesus there is hope for humanity. Our task, as God's people, is to communicate the good news, knowing that forgiveness and restoration is available for all those who believe. This is the good news to be taken into every corner of the globe.

Conclusion

This basic understanding of our context helps us come to terms with risk and suffering. If we view the world as a *perfect* place, risk and suffering will confuse us. If we view the world as a *broken* place, risk and suffering will drive us to depression. But when we grasp the biblical reality that we are living in-between these two extremes, we develop a patient long-term view that will sustain us.

So although we live in the middle times and there is darkness around us – nevertheless, there is hope. We have work to do.

---

5   *Matthew 24: 14*
6   *1 John 5: 19*

For reflection and/or discussion on Chapter 1

1. In your own words, describe to someone else what the two "bookends" of human history are.
2. Life in-between the "bookends" means you are living among brokenness, pain, and frailty. Make a mental list of evidence where risk and suffering is going on in your own life; in the lives of others around you (i.e. family and friends); and in your community and the nation where you live or are going to live.

Questions

1. Have you arrived at a balance in your own mind about life between the "bookends" of history?
2. We know that God's "redemption project" began its implementation at the cross and that there is hope that one day, everything in creation will be brought together under the control of Christ. How does this make you feel about life and ministry in a world of risk and suffering?

Notes

Risk & Suffering in the Old Testament

"Everybody hurts…sometimes"

Michael Stipe, lead singer of R.E.M.

© Night Garden Music

Defining Risk and Suffering

The word 'risk' is defined as an action which exposes the risk-taker to the possibility of danger. By taking a risk we expose ourselves – or others – to the possibility of physical harm, financial loss, or some other unpleasant consequence. We will define the word 'suffering' as the consequence of such risk. So risk and suffering are really two sides of the same coin. By taking a risk we expose ourselves to the possibility of suffering.

Having said this, risk is an unavoidable element in life because, as we have seen, in a fallen world we are frail and subject to disease, accident, difficulty and a million other dangers. These days we go to extraordinary lengths to eliminate risk, despite the self-evident futility because risk and suffering can never be totally eliminated.

> We go to extraordinary lengths to eliminate risk but risk and suffering can never be totally eliminated

In his excellent book *Risk is Right*, John Piper says risk is unavoidable because only God knows the future:

> *"[As God] knows the outcome of all his actions before they happen, he plans accordingly. His omniscience rules out the very possibility of taking risks. But not so with us. We are not God; we are ignorant."* [7]

Without knowing what the future holds, we cannot totally avoid risk. We urge each other to 'take care' or 'play it safe'. Our culture prioritises Health and Safety as though the sole aim of human existence is to arrive safely at death. In fact, risk-avoidance has entered our theology in that one school of thinking – the *Prosperity Gospel* – states that God's intention for his people is only for their happiness and wealth. In the words of Joel Osteen:

---

7   *'Risk is Right'*, John Piper, p.18

"It's God's will for you to live in prosperity instead of poverty", and "If you want success, if you want to be prosperous and healthy, you must boldly declare words of faith and victory over yourself".[8]

The idea here is that prosperity – i.e. financial and physical – is God's intention and that any form of suffering is against God's will or a sign of sin or failure. At best this is a half-truth in that God does want the best for us; however, it's profoundly unbiblical to say God wants our lives to be problem-free.

Biblical characters were also living in these "middle times" in a world fractured by sin. They, like us, were fallible human beings, endowed with free will, unable to predict the future and therefore forced to take risks. Let's look at a few Old Testament characters to see how risk and suffering played out in their experience.

Gideon

Picture the scene. A huge army of ferocious soldiers turn up in your country. They ravage the land, steal livestock, terrorise civilians and force them to live in the mountains. The solution? To find the weakest tribe in the land, choose the puniest member of that tribe, then sent most of the already-outnumbered army home. Only then did they go into battle, which sounds crazy but it's what God did with Gideon in Judges 6 and 7 where he explains why:

"You have too many men. I cannot deliver Midian into their hands, or Israel boast against me, 'My own strength has saved me' ". [9]

It is through using weak "risk-takers" that God's power is able to shine through

The story of Gideon reveals an important aspect of God's character: he is glorified through weakness. It's through using weak people that his power is able to shine through. If a vast army of ferocious warriors had won the victory, nobody would have noticed – it would be entirely normal – but for a tiny army, led by a weedy, nervous young man, to defeat the Midianites meant they had a powerful God. God's kingdom seems upside-down to our minds: weakness is strength; a puny man is a mighty warrior; risk is safety.

David

David was not kingly material. His dad didn't even bother to call him for interview when Samuel popped round for a chat. Talk about inauspicious beginnings! Yet David was the only man

---

8   Joel Osteen, 'Your Best Life Now'
9   Judges 7:2

described by God as 'a man after my own heart'; [10] he became head of a royal dynasty in Israel and was the writer of the Psalms.

We may be surprised that God chooses people so weak. But God deliberately chooses insignificant people in order to demonstrate his own power. As God says: *"The Lord does not look at the things people look at. People look at the outward appearance, but the Lord looks at the heart".*[11]

David lived a wild life of risk and joy, whether on the run from Saul, hiding in caves, or winning victories against the odds. His Psalms oscillate between uncontainable delight and abject despair. He knew suffering and he knew joy. Without risk his life would have gone nowhere.

> Suffering saints recognise that heaven is worth more than earth.

Daniel

Daniel risked his life for God – and suffered as a result. This came about as a result of his refusal to compromise his faith by bowing down to Nebuchadnezzar's idol or to the emperor Darius. This was not so much risky as downright suicidal. Yet it reveals a vital aspect of following God. Our life on earth is less important than our relationship with God. Life, though a precious gift, pales into insignificance compared to the glory of eternity with God.

This simple truth has motivated every Christian martyr from Stephen in Acts 8, to the modern day. Suffering saints have recognised that what's in store for us is worth more than what is currently around us; heaven is worth more than earth. The delight that awaits us is worth any suffering we might be called to endure. It is written of Jesus: "who, for the joy that was set before him, endured the cross…".[12] Daniel faced death twice – not because he was foolhardy, but because he knew the joy that was awaiting him.

Nehemiah

Things were going well for Nehemiah; he was a trusted advisor to the Persians, the superpower of their day. He was also well paid and highly respected, yet he chose to resign, travel to a desolate and ruined part of the Middle East, and rebuild the city of Jerusalem in the face of hostility from locals and his own people. He and his colleagues rebuilt the walls of Jerusalem in constant fear of attack, without any outside assistance, and far from any potential source of help.

---

10   *Acts 13:22*
11   *1 Samuel 16:7*
12   *Hebrews 12:2*

A bit risky, you might think; unwise even. Yet under his leadership the work was completed, the exiles returned, the law was read and the Israelites recommitted themselves to God. He understood the risks and knew fear, but his zeal for God was greater than the dangers around him.

Jeremiah

Here's a challenging thought. Suffering doesn't always lead to a pleasant outcome. When God called Jeremiah he told him: 'They will fight against you, but they shall not prevail against you'[13].

Jeremiah's brothers betrayed him; he was beaten, imprisoned, threatened with death and eventually dumped in a disused water cistern. He ended his life in exile in Egypt. It's hard to imagine how he could have suffered more – and yet nothing good seemed to come of it.

Except, that is, for his unfailing obedience to God. How many of us would have remained steadfast in the face of such difficulty? God came first despite what life threw at Jeremiah. What a model of faithfulness.

For reflection and/or discussion on Chapter 2

1. With risk and suffering being so "normal" among people God used in the Bible, is this a new thought for you?
2. If mission history has seen God's power shine more effectively through weak "risk-takers", in what way has the chapter challenged your relationship to risk?

Questions

We have said that suffering saints 'recognise that heaven is worth more than earth'.

1. How true is this of you – which is more real to you, earth or heaven?
2. Why do you think this might be?

---

13   Jeremiah 1:19

Risk & Suffering in the New Testament

"A ship is safe in harbour, but that's not what ships are for".
William G.T. Shedd

Jesus: His Life

Throughout his life, Jesus knew hidden suspicion and outright hostility. As a toddler he was persecuted by Herod who, in his insane jealousy, massacred children in an attempt to kill Jesus. He was nearly stoned to death when he first preached in his home town. He was harassed throughout his ministry by people trying to catch him out in order to accuse him of blasphemy.

He declined when urged to seize power from the Romans, choosing instead to subject himself to their authority. He entered Jerusalem not on a warhorse as a conquering hero, but on a donkey, the symbol of humility. The crowds that shouted "Hosanna!" one day screamed "Crucify!" two days later. His best friends deserted him; one of them betrayed him. He was beaten, tortured, and executed alongside common criminals.

Yet the Bible describes his life as a victory! *"And having disarmed the powers and authorities, he made a public spectacle of them, triumphing over them by the cross".* [14]

Without reservation, Jesus embraced the risk of attack. He was betrayed; abandoned and frequently suffered. Jesus lived, ministered, risked, suffered and died – this triggered a resurrection and victory.

And we are called to copy him:

"Whoever claims to live in him must live as Jesus did" [15]
"Follow my example, as I follow the example of Christ" [16]
"In your relationships with one another, have the same mindset as Christ Jesus" [17]
"To this you were called, because Christ suffered for you, leaving you an example that you should follow in his steps." [18]

14 Colossians 2:15
15 1 John 2:6
16 1 Corinthians 11:1
17 Philippians 2:5
18 1 Peter 2:21

Jesus is the supreme example for us all to follow. We are to emulate his teaching, his attitude, and behaviour – including his openness to risk and suffering.

Jesus: The Two Kingdoms

Throughout his life Jesus modelled a value system that is radically opposed to ours. He calls us to love our enemies; to bless those who want to harm us; to put aside our defences and refuse to fight back. In his world, a mite given by a penniless widow is more money than a wealthy man. To Jesus, we are blessed when we mourn and are persecuted; a man from a hated religious minority is our neighbour; if you lose your life you find it; if you save your life you lose it; the first are last and the last first.

These are the values of the kingdom of God and are radically different to our society. What seems like victory in the kingdom of God may look like defeat on earth – and vice versa. What may seem like common sense on earth may look like lunacy in the kingdom of God – and vice versa. Jesus goes so far as to say: *"What is exalted among men is an abomination in the sight of God".* [19]

> Suffering is not a possibility but instead an inevitable consequence for followers of Jesus

When we adopt this value system as followers of Jesus we set ourselves against this world. Jesus systematically turned his back on everything that this world holds dear: money, family, possessions, security, even life itself. Suffering was the inevitable result. He warned his followers on numerous occasions they would need to be ready to do the same:

"You will be hated by everyone because of me". [20]

"Then you will be handed over to be persecuted and put to death, and you will be hated by all nations because of me" [21]

"If the world hates you, keep in mind that it hated me first" [22]

"If they persecuted me, they will persecute you also" [23]

"The time is coming when anyone who kills you will think they are offering a service to God" [24]

"In this world you will have trouble." [25]

---

19   Luke 16:15
20   Matthew 10:22
21   Matthew 24:9
22   John 15:18
23   John 15:20
24   John 16:2
25   John 16:33

The odd thing is not that Christians around the world are persecuted, but that so many of us are surprised when persecution occurs. The world is enemy territory as C. S. Lewis put it:

> *"Enemy-occupied territory---that is what this world is. Christianity is the story of how the rightful king has landed, you might say landed in disguise, and is calling us to take part in a great campaign of sabotage."* [26]

This world is broken by sinful hearts and social structures. As followers of Jesus we are called to engage with it in the love and grace of Jesus. In doing so we'll be setting ourselves against this world as we set our sights on a higher world:

> *"If you belonged to the world, it would love you as its own. As it is, you do not belong to the world, but I have chosen you out of the world. That is why the world hates you."* [27]

We are called to be different (a root meaning of holy). This tends to lead to suffering as Jesus makes clear. He doesn't say "you may have trouble", he says "you will have trouble". Suffering is not a mere 'possibility' but an 'inevitability' in a broken world.

Christians will suffer, not just because of the inherent difficulty of human existence – after all, non-Christians get cancer and die in car accidents too – but also because they have been commanded to set themselves against the standards of the world.

Paul

Another person who was committed to the 'sabotage mission' described by C. S. Lewis was Paul of Tarsus. A vicious persecutor of the early church, Paul witnessed the martyrdom of Stephen and was on his way to Damascus to persecute more followers of Jesus, when God intervened. He was prayed for by Ananias – a Christian who also took a risk to do so – and this changed Paul's life.

In the course of his ministry Paul was beaten, jailed, stoned, put on trial, flogged, and abused. He was harassed all over Asia Minor, became shipwrecked on Malta where he clambered onto dry land only to have a viper bite his hand. He ended up being beheaded on the orders of the Roman Emperor Nero.

Yet Paul is the man who wrote half of the New Testament; shepherded the early churches across Asia Minor, evangelised and preached to thousands of people in the most challenging

---

26 *C. S. Lewis, "Mere Christianity".*
27 *John 15:19*

of circumstances. The man who, in his letter to the church in Rome, wrote: *"I consider that the suffering of this present time are not worth comparing with the glory that is to be revealed to us."*[28]

Paul's example is one of wild-eyed dedication to the purposes of God, a radical refusal to submit to the standards of this world and a total commitment to the cause of Jesus set him at odds with the Roman Empire and he knew it: *"Do not be conformed to this world, but be transformed by the renewal of your mind…".*[29]

> Paul didn't search for suffering but when it came as a result of making Jesus known he thought Jesus was worth it

Paul didn't deliberately seek out suffering. On one occasion he fled from it by being lowered from the walls of Damascus in a basket. He also fled from Iconium when he and Barnabas discovered a plot to kill him. For Paul, suffering was not something you go searching for, but something which comes about as a result of a total abandonment to making Jesus known – he calculated that Jesus was worth it!

Revelation

Revelation is a rich and strange vision, given to the Apostle John during his exile on the island of Patmos. It's full of exotic imagery, dramatic events and symbolic language. However, its depiction of suffering is vital to our understanding of this topic. It's here, at the end of all things and the culmination of history, that we are given a glimpse of the deeper purpose in suffering which so many of God's people have had to endure throughout AD history. Writers such as Paul, Peter and James encouraged their readers to remain faithful under suffering because of the glory that awaits believers in Jesus – it is the glory that is revealed in the book of Revelation.

In chapter 6, when the seals on the scroll are opened, a group of martyrs call out to God for justice against those who killed them. The response they receive is striking. A certain number of martyrs will be called before the end comes:

> *"Then they were each given a white robe and told to rest a little longer, until the number of their fellow servants and their brothers should be complete, who were to be killed as they themselves had been."* [30]

Then a multitude are seen dressed in white, from all the nations, praising God and an elder asks John who they are and then answers his own question:

---

28 *Romans 8:18*
29 *Romans 12:2*
30 *Revelation 6:11*

"These are the ones coming out of the great tribulation. They have washed their robes and made them white in the blood of the Lamb.[31]"

These two visions view suffering from a different perspective – namely from the end of time looking back to now, rather than from now looking forwards. This enables us to see the end of the story and the reason for the persecution, which Satan has unleashed through history:

"Then the dragon became furious with the woman and went off to make war on the rest of her offspring, on those who keep the commandments of God and hold to the testimony of Jesus.[32]"

We also see the supreme victory of the faithful followers of God:

"They have conquered him [Satan] by the blood of the Lamb and by the word of their testimony, for they loved not their lives even unto death. Therefore rejoice…"[33]

These visions may seem bizarre but they are comforting. The glory, which Stephen and Paul among other martyrs hoped for, is finally revealed; victory will be won. Death is not the end. Jesus is triumphant and Satan will be vanquished. Persecution, suffering, even death itself will become insignificant and devoid of power, in the face of the overwhelming victory of Christ.

Conclusion

The risks taken by biblical characters – Noah to Joseph, Gideon, Elijah, Job, Jonah, the disciples, Ananias, Paul, Stephen and many more – were based on a simple calculation. Their willingness to risk exposing themselves to danger was rooted in the belief that the greatness of God was worth it. Pain and suffering was made beautiful by God's promise of eternal life. As Jesus, the supreme risk-taker, himself said:

"Do not be afraid of those who kill the body but cannot kill the soul. Rather, be afraid of the One who can destroy both soul and body in hell.[34]"

Of course, all humans are exposed to suffering through sickness, accidents, bereavement and so on, but Christians *choose* to expose themselves to risk because of the biblical mandate to stand for righteousness in a broken world. Seen from this perspective, the Bible is a manual for

---

31 *Revelation 7:14*
32 *Revelation 12:17*
33 *Revelation 12:11-12*
34 *Matthew 10:28*

radical risk-takers. It's packed full of stories about the faithfulness of those who were made bold by love and the promise of heaven.

So why is it that our modern church is so afraid of risk? What went wrong?

For reflection and/or discussion on Chapter 3

1. The biblical position is that risk and suffering (in some form) is not a 'possibility' but an 'inevitability' for people who follow Jesus.
2. We have established that people in the Bible:

    i) didn't go looking for suffering;

    ii) sometimes took steps to avoid it;

    iii) but if it came as a result of making Jesus known, they thought it was worth it.

In what ways is this approach reasonable; balanced; biblical?

Questions

1. Do you accept the idea that the daily risks, which surround us, are an 'inevitable' part of life? If so why? If not, why not?
2. How has this material affected your thinking about suffering in your own life as a follower of Christ?
3. Do you think your love for God is sufficient (at this point) to make the risks you may face worthwhile?

Notes

Whatever happened to Risk?

"When Jesus calls a man, he bids him come and die".

The Cost of Discipleship, Dietrich Bonhoeffer

So the question is 'Whatever happened to risk and suffering in Christian thinking?' The early Christians had no problem with it; hundreds went to their deaths for refusing to bow down to pagan gods. One early theologian wrote a defiant letter to the authorities saying: *"We spring up in greater numbers the more we are mown down by you: the blood of the Christians is the seed of a new life".*[35]

Successive generations of Christians continued in their footsteps. Some missionaries to Africa in the 19th century packed their belongings in coffins and bought one-way tickets knowing they would probably not return. Yet down the centuries, when confronted with missionaries planning to go overseas, some Christians have responded by asking: "But is it *safe* to go there?"

This idea has gained ground in recent decades and we have got to the place where we assume Christian discipleship should be carried out with minimum risk or difficulty. This assumes that following Jesus is to be done pleasantly, safely and with no negative consequence for our well-being.

A recent study of how risk affects missionary families concluded:

> *"Evangelicals, on the whole, do not acknowledge the place of pain and suffering in a believer's discipleship and service. Further, Christians unconsciously promote an ideal of a comfortable, pain-free and worry-free existence. For missionaries in risky places, that kind of unbiblical idealism is not only wrong; it simply does not work".*[36]

So what went wrong?

---

35 *Tertullian, "Apologeticum", ch.50*
36 *Dwight Baker and Robert Priest in "The Missionary Family" (2014), p.35.*

The Risky Church

Clearly risk and suffering have been "normal" throughout church history as Christians of all denominations realised that to follow Christ is to set yourself against the world system, which can have negative consequences.

Disciples of Christ travelled, preached, founded churches, suffered and often died in gruesome ways. For example Polycarp, an early bishop of Smyrna (Turkey), was burned at the stake for refusing to burn incense to the Roman Emperor. Countless Christians were killed by the regime of the Roman Empire, including being devoured by wild animals; being left on an icy lake to freeze to death; crucified; and even coated in tar and set alight to provide illumination for Emperor Nero's garden parties.

Early Christians were not the only risk-takers; early missionaries to Europe entered a dark and violent continent, crossing oceans and rivers in leaky boats and preaching to violent pagan warlords, risking their lives to spread the gospel.

Monks later established monasteries, centres of Christian study and community, many of which were ravaged by the Vikings. Later on, missionaries travelled further into dangerous territory to set up mission compounds, hospitals and other institutions – all at significant personal risk. Many were martyred in North America, China, Korea, Japan, and Africa.

This is not to suggest that the early church was universally bold or completely successful. Many were content to settle for a bland 'culturally Christian' existence, as is the case today. Yet every time the gospel has spread, it has been on the foundation of Christians who were prepared to take risks for the glory of God.

The Health & Safety Church

Today many western Christians have come to faith in an increasingly post-modern social environment that includes: Secular Humanism, Religious Pluralism and Consumerism. These powerful drivers influence modern western societies and colour the thinking of followers of Christ.

Secular Humanism is a 'non-theistic' belief system, which values human beings above everything else. Organised religion has been undermined by evolution theory and a scientistic view of the world since the 19th century onwards. It fosters the belief that humans can create a perfect world and determine their future so religion is seen as redundant.

The British Humanist Association insists: "We can live good lives without religious or superstitious beliefs". This is the opposite of the biblical view that God is pre-eminent and perfect while we human beings are neither.

The Humanist effect on the Christian attitude to risk is deadly because it shifts our focus from how we can serve God to how we can manipulate circumstances to ensure our own self-preservation. Our society is more concerned with risk assessments and the issues of 'Health & Safety' in a 'me-centred' world that seems incompatible with the 'God-centred' world of Christian discipleship.

Religious Pluralism is now an integral part of European cultures, where all religious truths are seen as equally valid. The West is increasingly seen as secular – although polls confirm that most westerners believe in a deity – but Christianity is just one religion among many, due to immigration and an increased global awareness of options which might help with the stresses of modern life, such as Buddhism. Increasing numbers of people are concluding that other religions are just alternative paths to God. A new strain of atheism is also increasing, thanks to the efforts of writers such as Richard Dawkins, Sam Harris and the late Christopher Hitchens.

As a result, belief in core Christian doctrines has declined. A poll in 2013 found that the number of American Christians who believe in the core biblical doctrines of heaven; hell; the devil; the virgin birth and the resurrection of Christ is in decline.[37] Due to 'political correctness', Christians are increasingly tentative about presenting the gospel to people from other spiritual traditions, in case they offend them.

Consumerism has developed in our western social environment which enjoys unparalleled wealth, together with improved technology. It's driven by a marketing industry that's skilled in the manipulation of people's aspirations. This has created a culture of greed and an addiction to possessions and the comforts of material wealth.

The more we have, the more we risk losing

During shopping sales such as 'Black Friday' someone was literally trampled to death in the rush to buy the latest flat-screen TV. In 2011 shoppers who were scrambling to be the first to reach cut-price goods actually stepped over the body of a man who was dying of a heart attack. This still goes on despite the fact that psychological surveys demonstrate that any link between wealth and happiness is a myth!

---

37 *Poll carried out by the Harris Company, December 2013.*

Consumerism affects mission recruitment as it fixes our eyes on the here and now rather than on Jesus and the hereafter. It also diverts money away from kingdom purposes. Jesus' command to go into the world – with all its risk and danger – is not easily received by people who are obsessed with possessions and money, which hold us back in an insidious way.

The more we have, the more we risk losing. Consumerism is an elegant trick of the enemy; if he can't crush the church with persecution he attempts to lull the western church to sleep with comfort and security – this seems to be working!

The Health & Safety Gospel

We also face the gospel of 'Health & Wealth', which is essentially the consumer mindset turned into a theology; but at least it's rejected by many Christians. However, the gospel of 'Health & Safety' is an equally insidious problem to which many Christians subscribe. This retains just enough of Jesus' teaching to be respectable, while any element of risk has been removed.

The cultural climate in which the western church exists prioritises safety and discourages risk. This distracts the church from its divine task of engaging with God in his world. If we let this happen, we become anaesthetised to such a degree that we become unable to engage in the spiritual conflict, which surrounds us.

It's not about us

So a common theme in our cultural context is that 'it's all about *us*'. This is conveyed through Secular Humanism, which tells us we can manage by ourselves; Religious Pluralism tells us that any 'truth' is true – as long as *we* believe it to be true; and Consumerism is an industry that's dedicated to the gratification of self. Our overwhelming priority is simply *us*: our own comfort, our own safety, our own happiness.

The biblical world view is the opposite. God is central and everything else comes second, which is why Jesus said: *"Whoever wants to be my disciple must deny themselves and take up his cross and follow me."* [38] and insists on the Old Testament command to *"'...love the Lord your God with all your heart and with all your soul and with all your mind and with all your strength.' The second is this: 'Love your neighbour as yourself'."* [39] So the goal of the church is to glorify *God*, not ourselves. We worship him, not ourselves; it's not about us but him; yet our culture loves anything more than it loves God – and we are in danger of swallowing the lie.

---

38 *Matthew 16:24*
39 *Mark 12:30-31*

For reflection and/or discussion on Chapter 4

1. There is an English proverb: 'Much wants more'. In this chapter we have said a similar thing using different words: 'The more we have, the more we risk losing.' In what ways are you aware of the negative effects of possessions and consumerism?

2. If Secular Humanism, Religious Pluralism and Consumerism influence the thinking of western followers of Christ, what examples of these influences can you recognise in your own Christian living?

Questions

1. How do you navigate your way around the consumer bug?

2. Risk surrounds us as a part of life but is our love for God sufficient to make the extra risk worthwhile – is this true of your life?

Notes

Radical Discipleship in a Risky World

The world is becoming an increasingly dangerous place – but it's also an exciting place. It can often feel as though we are reliving the famous phrase of Charles Dickens in *A Tale of Two Cities*: "*It was the best of times; it was the worst of times.*"

The Best of Times

A friend of mine once found himself sitting in a hotel room having lunch with a Christian. Pretty normal, you might think – except that this particular Christian had once been a vicious opponent of the church and had even volunteered to carry out an armed attack against it, even though he knew he would probably be killed in the process. On his way to carry out his mission he had a dream of Jesus who called him to follow him. He returned home and began to do just that. He is now working as an evangelist in an unreached part of the world.

The movements we see around the world in recent years have often been in the face of persecution.

For example:

- A century ago there was not a single church in Seoul, capital of South Korea. Today, seven of the world's ten largest churches are in Seoul; South Korea is the second largest missionary sending country in the world; some 30% of South Koreans are Christians. The cost of this was sporadic bouts of persecution which killed many of the first Korean Christians and some of the early missionaries.

- In 1900 there were around nine million Christians in Africa; today there are an estimated 400 million.

- In South America a similar phenomenon has occurred: from around 250,000 Christians in 1900 to over 60 million today – and that is just the Evangelicals.

- The growth of the church in Nepal; the tens of thousands of Iranians turning to Christ around the world; the flourishing of the church in regions of the world previously untouched by the gospel.

These are unprecedented events which no other generation in church history has seen.

Most thrilling of all is the fact that the church is now, for the first time in history, starting to resemble the vision of John in the Revelation chapter 7 where he saw a "*great multitude from every nation, tribe, people and language*" worshipping the Lamb.

The epicentre of the early church was the Mediterranean Sea. It then shifted to Europe; then to North America; and now it is moving to a number of regions in the global south – sub-Saharan Africa, Latin America, China and South-East Asia.

We are not there yet – there are still huge numbers of unreached people groups to be accessed with the gospel – but the situation in the world church is more rampant and diverse than it has ever been. What an exciting time to be alive!

The Worst of Times

Turmoil

And now for the bad news. Our world is becoming more fractured, violent and unequal. The great global alliances established during the 20th century – NATO, the UN, the EU – are coming under increasing pressure as countries prioritise their own self-interest. Nationalism is on the rise, which leads in many cases to increased xenophobia:

- In the 2014 European elections nationalist parties made huge gains in countries such as France, Denmark, the Netherlands, Hungary, Greece, and the UK.

- Suspicion and fear seem to dominate public discourse; mosques have been firebombed and daubed with graffiti in countries such as the UK, Sweden and Canada.

- Churches are being bombed in countries such as Pakistan, Nigeria, Kenya and Niger.

- Jewish centres have been attacked in France, Belgium and India.

Elsewhere there are increasing sectarian tensions between Sunni and Shi'a Muslims. Sectarian violence has become the norm in places such as Pakistan and Iraq. The Arab Spring caused an upheaval across the Middle East as protests toppled governments and new governments were installed, only to be toppled themselves, as was the case in Egypt and Libya.

Violence

The level of violence in the world is increasing:

- The September 11th attacks in the US stunned the world with footage of passenger aircraft being deliberately flown into buildings, murdering thousands of civilians.

- More recent atrocities carried out by the militants of the, so called, Islamic State and also the Taliban in Pakistan and Afghanistan has taken barbarity to new heights.

- Hostility has broken out on the borders of Europe as Russia and Ukraine are in conflict.

- Syria has been torn apart, with as many as 200,000 people killed and millions displaced.

- Communal violence in the Central African Republic killed thousands in late 2013.

- Opportunistic attacks are on the increase, most recently the Charlie Hebdo attacks in Paris and the Tunisian beach massacre in Sousse in 2015.

It is now recognised that violence against Christians has also increased: in 2013 the International Society for Human Rights calculated that 80% of all religious violence in the world is aimed at Christians. Attacks on churches in Iraq, Pakistan, Kenya, Nigeria and many other places have killed thousands in the last couple of years.

By 2016 the richest 1% of the world will possess more wealth than the remaining 99% put together

Inequality

There is a gaping void between rich and poor. The richest 20% of the world's population share 76% of its resources, while the poorest 20% share just 1.5%. According to UNICEF 22,000 children die every day from malnutrition and other preventable diseases. One billion people in the world are unable to read a book or to sign their own name.[40] Half of the world's children live in poverty. 80% of the world's population live in countries where the gap between rich and poor is increasing. A paper published by Oxfam stated that by 2016 the richest 1% of the world's population would possess more wealth than the remaining 99% put together.[41]

---

40 UNICEF Report, 'The State of the World's Children'.
41 Oxfam report, 'Having It All And Wanting More', published Jan 19th 2015.

If all those statistics are too much for you, consider this simple fact: more money is spent on ice cream in Europe every year than it would cost to provide basic education for everyone in the world – *everyone*.

In spite of all human 'progress' humankind has made in the last few centuries – the eradication of countless diseases; the provision of healthcare and social welfare; the protection of individual freedoms – the fact remains that for the vast majority of the world's inhabitants life is a struggle just to survive, while a small minority of westerners live in unparalleled comfort and safety. We have created a world in which dogs in Britain receive better food and healthcare than refugees in Somalia.

All this begs the question, shouldn't we all be *doing* something about it?

Radical Mission Today

So in the light of the biblical imperative to engage with God in his mission to salvage a broken world, how should we go about it?

Embrace Risk

First we need to realise that, in going into the world in the name of Jesus, who said, suffering *will* come, we take a calculated risk.

Risk comes in different forms wherever in the world we follow Christ – financial risk; the risk of damaging our professional prospects; the risk of losing our friends; the risk of living far from our family; the risk of being injured or even killed – but in whatever form it comes, we must be clear that risk *will* come. Risk is therefore a non-negotiable part of our Christian life. As the mission pioneer Hudson Taylor said: "Unless there is an element of risk in our exploits for God, there is no need for faith."

A pre-requisite is to have a mind-set that accepts the presence of risk. This changes the question from: 'Why should I take risks for Jesus?' to 'How can I *not* risk myself for Jesus?' Another mission pioneer, C. T. Studd, said: "If Jesus Christ be God and died for me, no sacrifice can be too great for me to make for him".

It's ironic that in a risk-averse society like ours, people are perfectly willing to take risks for the wrong reason – money. Take for example oil workers who travel to Libya or Algeria; or telecommunications engineers who go to war-torn regions of the world. People gladly move across the world to challenging countries in pursuit of tax-free salaries and company perks. And all the while comparatively few move to such countries to reach the lost.

Why is it that some take risks for money, while Christians can be reluctant to take risks for God? Is Jesus less precious than a new oil well or a mobile phone contract?

Prioritise the greatest need

Disciples of Christ are called to be risky people who do risky things in risky places. This is not because risk is in itself a good thing but because the risky places are also the places of greatest need. Church denominations report that it's easier to appoint ministers for the leafy suburbs than for the tough inner-city neighbourhoods.

In the same way, it's harder to recruit mission workers for Kyrgyzstan than it is for Thailand. I recently heard a conference speaker comment wryly on the challenges of recruiting people for difficult countries, saying: "*It's amazing how God is calling so many people to holiday destinations and so few to the slums of Calcutta*". Globally speaking he has a point. The number of missionaries working with unreached people groups is minimal; roughly one worker for every 250,000 people.

Unnecessary risk
is precisely that –
"unnecessary"

The heroes of the Christian faith are heroes - precisely because they went to the areas of greatest need: George Muller with the orphans of Bristol; William Carey in 19th century India; Brother Andrew to Communist Eastern Europe (and now the most volatile parts of the Muslim world) or Jackie Pullinger who went to the gangland of the Hong Kong drug lords.

James Gilmour, one of the first missionaries to Mongolia, said: "I thought it reasonable that I should seek to work where the work was most abundant and the workers fewest". We need to have the same attitude if the gospel is to penetrate the *whole* world and not just the 'safe' parts.

Risk Management

While we need to be aware of the probability of suffering this doesn't mean we are called to be reckless. Unnecessary risk is precisely that – 'unnecessary'. We need to find a balance between excessive risk and excessive safety. The key is wise stewardship. Everything we have comes from God and we are called to manage it wisely, whether it's possessions, money, time or our lives.

There are plenty of biblical examples to guide us. For example:

- Nehemiah took risks but he was also wise when he chose not to confront his opponents (Chapter 6) knowing that they wanted to do him harm.
- David took risks but he also fled to the Philistines (1 Sam. 27) knowing that Saul would kill him if he could, prompting him to leave the situation for a period of time.
- The Apostle Paul routinely took risks, but he also fled Damascus by night to avoid persecution (Acts 9) and again in Iconium (Acts 14) when a crowd gathered to kill him.

This does not mean we should instantly flee at the first sign of trouble – all of these men faced dangers at other times yet chose not to run. However, we should recognise that times will come when a strategic retreat is a viable option – 'discretion being the greater part of valour'.

Mission workers, even those working in dangerous countries, routinely aim to manage risk appropriately. We are trained in how to secure our homes; how to be aware of potential hijackers when driving; how to respond if we are affected by grenade attacks, shootings, or suicide bombs; how to respond if we are kidnapped. While this training is a "reasonable" precaution, it cannot deter unnecessary risk.

We also plan our movements on a risk/benefit analysis, which asks: 'Does the benefit of a particular activity outweigh the risks?' Once a religious cleric called me and asked if he could come and meet me to discuss the Bible. I could have said no – but the opportunity seemed to be a good one, so I suggested we meet in a public place, where the risk was less. The meeting turned out to be very worthwhile indeed.

Another time I was invited to speak to a group of Muslim missionaries in a mosque in an area of town I knew to be unsafe, and at night. I chose not to go. Was it cowardly of me? Or was it a prudent calculation of risk and benefit? I don't know, but we always pray for wisdom in knowing how to manage our movements as a routine part of ministry in a context of risk and suffering.

The risk of *not* going

We have looked at the risks that Christians take when they choose to go into the world to minister as 'lambs among wolves'. It is also worth considering the other side of the coin: what are the risks of *not* going?

If we do go, we will be exposing ourselves to risk, ridicule, injury, discomfort, separation from our loved ones, possibly death. Yet through us, people may come to hear about the world-transforming love of Jesus.

If we do *not* go, people living in darkness will *not* 'see a great light', but will instead continue to live – and die – in darkness.

Is our personal safety worth that much?

For reflection and/or discussion on Chapter 5

1. It is often said in Christian circles: 'The blood of the saints is the seed of the church'. Do you think there is a correlation between suffering and extraordinary church growth? What other ways can you think of, which might also prompt such growth?

2. We have seen that the richest 1% of the world possess more wealth than the remaining 99% put together.

   When seen first-hand, abject poverty can be a shock to western Christians. How might ministering to people in the context of the following forms of suffering affect you:

   i)   adult beggars?

   ii) intentionally maimed child beggars?

   iii) street children?

   iv) the sex-trafficked?

Question

While some take risks overseas for money, Christians can be reluctant to take risks for God. How would you explain this?

The Joy of Discipleship

"But we never can prove the delights of His love
Until all on the altar we lay;
For the favour He shows, for the joy He bestows,
Are for those who will trust and obey."

John Sammis

Much of what we have said so far may come across as gloomy; even depressing. In writing about suffering there is a possibility of over-emphasising the negative aspects of discipleship. It's certainly vital for the western church to come to terms with the reality of our role, as Christians, in a broken world and also to recognise that suffering can be a consequence if we choose to engage with it as Jesus commanded us to do. Yet this shouldn't hide the simple truth put to us by Dietrich Bonhoeffer in his book *The Cost of Discipleship*: 'Discipleship is joy'.

Count It All Joy, My Brothers

My wife's parents served as mission workers in India and Pakistan for nearly twenty years. During that time they faced a number of difficulties. For instance, my father-in-law was diagnosed with cancer, and once an ammunition dump near their house blew up, forcing them to escape on foot as rockets and mortar shells landed around them. They also faced constant stress and incessant hostility; he was fired from his job and publically disgraced because he refused to take bribes. Most painfully, one of their daughters (my wife's sister) contracted leukaemia and died just before her third birthday.

When I first met him I asked him how he had kept going through such difficult times. "*Oh*", he said. "*I'd do it again in a heartbeat. We had a blast*".

Other missionaries come to the same conclusion:

- Samuel Zwemer was a 20th century missionary to the Middle East. He worked there for his entire life and saw almost no visible success. While there both of his daughters died within eight days of each other. Later in life he looked back and said: *"The sheer joy of it comes back. Gladly I would do it all again…"*.

- The dying words of David Brainerd, an early American missionary, who ministered alone and died young were these: *"I declare, now I am dying, I would not have spent my life otherwise for the whole world."*

- Alexander Mackay, an early missionary to Uganda who died of malaria at a young age: *"It is no sacrifice, as some think, to come here as pioneers of Christianity and of civilization. I would not give my position here for all the world."*

I was once listening to a Ugandan Christian describe his journey to faith. Born into a Muslim family, he was a violent persecutor of the church, until he heard the audible voice of God while praying and came to faith as a result. He narrowly escaped with his life when men tried to hunt him down with knives and guns. When I asked him how he felt after moving to the UK he almost seemed wistful, as though he missed the good old days: "*God was very close to me in the difficult times. Now that I'm living in safety, I don't feel his presence as closely. Perhaps that's because I don't need to….*"

The Ups and the Downs

There is a deep and rich joy in risky Christian discipleship, journeying through ups and downs; the 'downs' only serve to make the 'ups' even more wonderful.

- Being separated from loved ones is hard; being reunited with them gives intense happiness.

- Living in an unchurched country is hard; returning home to a church full of worshipping Christians feels almost miraculous.

- Putting up with power cuts, water shortages and limited food supplies makes you appreciate those resources even more.

- Walking the kids down the road to play in a western play park may not sound like much but after several years in a confined environment with innumerable security restrictions, it's a significant blessing to us.

- After three years in Asia my family returned to the UK for a break. I spent much of it walking through the lush English countryside, simply because I had forgotten how wonderful green grass is.

So the 'ups' are not possible without 'downs'. Our appreciation of the good things is deepened by life's challenges; and without experiencing the difficult aspects of life we can't truly appreciate the God-given richness in life.

Seen this way, suffering is not the opposite of joy but the means of unlocking it. This is life to the max – answers to prayer; miracles; crushing defeats; soaring triumphs; pain and sorrow and immense joy – this is rich indeed.

What, after all, is the alternative? To drift quietly through life, playing it safe, in order to arrive peacefully at death? Is that really the 'life in all its fullness' Jesus came to give us? We may well choose to play it safe – we may even succeed in keeping our earthly lives intact until retirement – but surely we would have to ask ourselves whether such a bland and banal existence, is worthy of the world-conquering God we profess to follow.

US President Theodore Roosevelt spoke powerfully about a life of struggle and risk in a passage worth quoting in full:

> *"The credit belongs to the man who is actually in the arena, whose face is marred by dust and sweat and blood; who strives valiantly; who errs, who comes short again and again, because there is no effort without error and shortcoming… but who does actually strive to do the deeds; who knows great enthusiasms, the great devotions; who spends himself in a worthy cause; who at the best knows in the end the triumph of high achievement, and who at the worst, if he fails, at least fails while daring greatly, so that his place shall never be with those cold and timid souls who neither know victory nor defeat."* [42]

We must present Christ in local clothes, stripped of western culture that has developed around him.

Again, this does not mean that all of us should head overseas. The notion that true discipleship has to lead to overseas mission work is faulty. Many of us are called to remain in our own context – as long as we are doing so out of a sense of calling and not out of a desire to avoid risk.

Neither should we over-balance the other way in a search for self-gratification. We don't embrace risky discipleship for the fun of it. The aim isn't to have a wild and interesting life or to store up interesting anecdotes. The aim is to glorify the risen Lord, making him known in his world. God, in his unimaginable grace, makes the journey thrilling. He is no slave driver. His yoke is 'easy' and his 'burden is light'; following in his footsteps is joyous.

---

42 *Citizenship in a Republic', speech given at the Sorbonne, Paris, on April 23rd 1910.*

Final Thoughts

In the course of these pages I have argued that risk and suffering are broadly misunderstood by the western church, which lacks a clear 'theology of suffering'. Without it, we become conditioned by our society to view any form of risk as abnormal and to be avoided.

This reduces our willingness to engage meaningfully with our broken world. The consequence is that the church of Jesus Christ in the West is in danger of selling its birth-right of reaching the world and accepted the substitute role as an impotent spectator, watching mutely from the side-lines while oppression and inequality are given free rein to dominate the world God loves.

We have also established that risk and suffering are an inevitable consequence of following Jesus. This is because his standards oblige us to be different (i.e. holy) and to set ourselves against the prevailing standards of this world.

We know that the perfection which awaits us is far greater than any difficulty we may experience now. Jesus is our supreme example of what it means to exchange temporary anguish for permanent joy. The writer of Hebrews exhorts us to:

> *"Fix our eyes on Jesus, the founder and perfecter of our faith, who for the joy that was set before him endured the cross, despising the shame, and is seated at the right hand of the throne of God".[43]*

A church that is timid and tentative, a church that puts personal safety first, will be incapable of bringing transformation to an increasingly fractured world. A church that is so entranced by possessions and comfort, by TV soaps and touchscreen trinkets, by career advancement and bank accounts, cannot truly be described as 'Christian'. It will have forfeited its right to use the name of Christ to describe itself.

We cease to be authentically 'Christian' if we allow our fear of suffering to prevent us from ministering to the broken-hearted, since it will demonstrate that we are totally out of step with the sacrificial God who gave himself for us and utterly unworthy of following in the triumphant footsteps of the sacrificial Christian pioneers who, in a few centuries of joyous toil, turned an apparently irrelevant offshoot of Judaism into the single largest faith movement in the world.

Finally – if we will set aside personal comfort; if we will embrace the risks of following Christ, we will become a transformative influence in the world through him.

---

43 *Hebrews 12:2*

By taking risks and by making ourselves weak, we enable God to demonstrate his strength through our weakness. This is the strength that conquered the powerful Midianites through the weakness of Gideon; it's also the strength that transformed the Roman Empire through the weakness of the early church.

It is this strength that transformed Fiji because James Calvert ignored advice and got off the ship in 1830. Embracing such risky weakness is, perhaps perversely, the most joyous experience in the world. The choice is ours. The world is waiting. A great cloud of witnesses is watching.

Let's do it!

For reflection and/or discussion on Chapter 6

1. 'If we will set aside our reliance on personal comfort and embrace the calculated risks that come with following Jesus, we will become a transformative influence in the world through him.'
   How far do you agree – or disagree – that the sentence above is a key part of the message of this book?
2. Are there any other headlines that stood out for you?

Questions

1. Risk is a non-negotiable part of life, but is your love for God sufficient to make intentional calculated risks for the gospel worth the while?
2. What steps will you now take to adjust any fear of risk in your life?

Notes

kitab
Interserve resources